A PACKET OF VERSE

A PACKET OF VERSE

By

Caroline Molyneux

Illustrations by Sally Griffith

THE GOLDEN QUILL PRESS
Publishers
Francestown   New Hampshire

Library of Congress Catalog Card Number 90-84877

ISBN 0-8233-0471-X

Printed in the United States of America

For My Family
John, Louise, Kate, William and Sarah

CONTENTS

A PACKET OF VERSE

ET TU?

On leafy limb above the ground
From human eye, near hidden,
Life abounds.
Burrows in the ground,
Hides in stonewall and all around.

The lake, the sea,
The river and canal are free
To flow.
And yet to you
I must quiet gently go.

A circle which no eye can find
Of finest thread,
Keeps you in mind.
A feel divine.
A hidden peace.
All this I've found
To you I'm bound.
Et vous?

Et tu?

HANDS

His hands are large.
His hands are strong; yet
Gentle hands you'd trust
Could do no wrong.

Hands that can a table make,
Hands that bread most ably bake.
Hands that can fashion a guitar,
Hands that strum a tune or pluck a bar.

Seaman's hands that knots can tie.
Doctor's hands to soothe a baby's cry.
The hands to hold me,
To caress me, to belong.
In those hands my future I do give,
The hands with whom I choose to live.

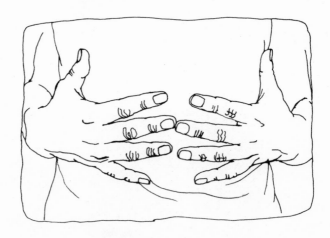

THE NATURAL WAY

The garden had been forgotten.
For years no interfering hand with nature's plan.
No clipping, no digging, no pruning, no mowing . . .
Just growing, and growing, and growing and
   growing . . .
A joyful wilderness.

Flower beds strident with purple willow herb on the
   march.
Roses, stalky tall, trying to compete.
Over all humming summer bees replete.
Once naked stone paved paths are ivy dressed.
Dandelions proud, yellow-helmeted stand guard.

A bird bath moss-grown, greenly stagnant,
The axis of activity.
Realm of birds, feathers water sprinkle, beaks dipped.
Tangle of convolvulus watches the patterns of flight,
Pink trumpets blowing a welcoming call.

Trim lawn, parade ground neat, no longer shorn;
A field of grasses; wheat, red-gemmed with poppies,
Waving free. The scented breeze making kites of the
   butterflies.
Protector of this plot, unruly privet hedge.
No regimented bush.
Sprouting branches proclaiming pride of ownership.
Oak and ash, watching, tall.

Sentinel.

ICE CREAM VENDOR

He stood on Manhattan street
In August heat.
His sign read
I SELL GOOD HUMOR.
An ice cream
Should she have vanilla or a choc?
"What can I do fe yer?" he asked.
Hesitant she stands and thinks.
Should she take a cone or bar?
"Oh! lady make up yer fucking mind . . .
The're people waiting right behind."

Good

SQUIRREL

Sassy squirrel under a tree,
Tail curled stares at me,
Sipping on my cup of tea.
"How about some nuts or bread?
Are you hoping to be fed?"
At the sound of my voice
He quickly fled. . . .
Straight up the tree.
Oh! how I wish that I could climb
To that leafy canopy sublime.

DEER

In the woods today
I met a herd of deer.
From me they fled.
Rocking motion, tails
White-side held high.
How could I tell them
Not to fear.
"I have no gun,
I would not hurt a one.
You are God's creatures
And like me have just
As much right to be here."

16

THOUGHT BEFORE A JOURNEY

On my sweaty jog today,
An oil tanker nearly plowed me down.
I thought I want the biggest funeral in town.
Buf if the DC10 crashes in the sea,
The whole wide world will know,
But not it's ME!

ON BRITISH RAIL

On the train,
Countryside rushing by,
Expectations riding high.
The modern road to meet my swain.
I need the comfort of his arms again.
Passing Hungerford, 'The Horse and Plough'.
The buffet car is open now.
A cup of tea, I need a snack.
Grope, swaying go two coaches back.
Fields of grazing sheep,
Playful lambs on hillocks leap.
Baroque clouds gild by sun.
Newbury, money to be won.
Ruffled ponds and mallard ducks.
The sun and cloud play nip and tucks.
The lady opposite deeply sucks
Her tea, rocking train spills over me.
Rainbow arches over spire.
Cows by gate bogged deep in mire.
Swiss rolls of hay quite careless lay,
Great houses from a previous day.
Suburban streets, cars and shops.
On platform number six we stop.
London chaos, umbrellas hide
Commuters scurrying, a taxi ride.
Homeward bound, the workers round.
I have still to break fresh ground.
Kings Cross, long ticket line,
No worry, plenty of time.

18

We ride the night,
The city lights recede,
Speeding train our trusty steed.
Growing dark, commuters weary,
Papers drop, their eyes are bleary.
Relaxing warmth and human smell.
Commuters sleep, I nod as well.
6:30 reaching Grantham Station.
I need the lav. and the wash basin.
Can I disturb the next door seat?
Or struggle past him to my feet.
Main stop, most passengers go forth.
In empty train still speeding north.
Dearest, for this I've waited hours.
Your greeting with a bunch of flowers.

HEARTBREAK

Oh! how I wanted you to say,
"Stay, stay my love, stay, stay."
But the words I needed
I never heard.
And so I went away.

ON RECEIVING AN EMPTY PACKET OF SEEDS

Dear Samuel Dobie,

We are writing to protest.
You claim your pansies are the best!
But here's the real croaker,
You sent a seedless packet of 'JOKER'.
Regretfully growers,

A pair of would be pansy sowers.

Good

WHIMSY

You are gentle.
You are strong.
With you I feel
That I belong.
And should we have
A second life?
I hope you'd choose me
For your wife.

Good

AUTUMN

In England there is autumn.
Bonfires, shining conkers,
Brussels sprouts.

In America there is the fall.
Maple leaves proclaim—
Red, orange, yellow shouts.

In Equatorial Africa
There is none of this at all.

Good

TO A DAUGHTER IN CHICAGO

What is a daughter?

A daughter is your delight
And your despair.
At school she is very bright.
Why is she always washing her hair?

A chubby, blonde bombshell at three
Who you cuddle on your knee.
A teenage raiser of hell,
To whom there is nothing you can tell.
She makes you scream and yell.
"Get out of the shower."

A party goer,
Home at four.
Worry some more.

A student at college,
Out west.
A charmer, a flirt.
Her visiting Dad's date,
The best.
For him out of jeans
And into a skirt.

She's beautiful and kind,
Rarely out of your mind.
Needs money—some more!
What does she use it for?

In the future, whatever you choose,
We, as your parents, can never lose
The joy of your being OUR GIRL.
We are proud to state,
"This is our daughter, Kate."

ON A BRIEF VISIT TO AUSTRIA

A tiny country—prosperous—
Clean and neat in every street.
National costumes worn with pride—
On bus or train an honour ride.

Fast flowing Salzach—chestnut lined.
Schloss guarded slopes, terraced and vined.
Here Richard Coeur de Lion was interred
Until Blondel's freeing song he heard.

Hellbrun—garden of playful fountain.
Swaying cable car up Untersberg mountain.
Exploding guns cross Salzburg—round after round—
St. Rupert's Day proclaims the sound.

Mozart country—Fuschl Lake.
Sacher torte most delicious cake.
The Danube—lunch on board—
A monastery at Melk we toured.

Vienna musical city of Strauss.
The glorious State Opera House.
Teatime concerts in the parkdt,
The city's magic after dark.

The mighty Hof—a nation's past—
Of royalty whose power didn't last.
Baroque churches, ornate, to heaven climb.
Demel's for pastries, gluttony a second time.

These are just minutest bits
Of what is known as Osterlitz.

PEACE

Each day blends into another . . .
Where does time go?
My past so far away . . .
Yet it was only yesterday.

My birth country, familiar ways.
English fields and English days.

Horizon blending sky, sea and sand.
We walk, we talk, we touch a hand.
Content . . .
When day is done we close our door,
To tell the world, "impinge no more."

A HOMEMAKER'S LAMENT

It is tough being a housewife.
You gear your life to their activity
You become a non-entity.
You are D's wife or P's ma,
You lose your own identity.

And everywhere you drive the car!

Daughter in your room when you want to dress.
Husband hands you his shirt to press.
"Hon, where are my socks?"
"Mom, where's my coat?"
You're the keeper of the family trivia.

And everywhere you drive the car!

Fill the lunch box, hope it won't go to waste.
One peanut butter, one salami, one for ham.
Rush to school bus in disorderly haste
Grabbing their homework, hear the door slam.
"See ya, Ma. Have a good trip, Pa."

And everywhere you drive the car!

On the 'phone when you need to call.
They've been together all that day
What ever do they find to say?

To their friends for a movie date,
Across the town, to walk, too far.

And everywhere you drive the car!

Why do all their things end up on the floor?
Why do they never close a door?
Take a shower that lasts an hour?
In the clothes you want to wear,
Leave them dirty—"Is that some tar?"

And everywhere you drive the car!

Meet them in the rain
From choir or football or ballet practice.
Drive him to the train.
Meet him at the airport—the plane is late.
An hour to wait. Should you try the bar?

And everywhere you drive the car!

Week-end comes. They're sleeping late,
The breakfast dishes until lunchtime wait.
"A coke! You're not going to eat?"
"Don't want food in all this heat.
Mom, take me to the pool, I told Jen we'd meet."

Get out the car, back in the chauffeur's seat!

You need some help to cut the grass,
You need some help to wash the car.
You leave the vacuum in their room,
Invitingly you prop up the broom.
No one heeds your plea,
They're too enthralled by the TV.

Now they drive your car.

They turn your order into chaos.
But when they've left
How you feel the loss.
The end of motherhood.
You're bereft.

HAZARDS OF A JOGGER

I jog at steady pace,
Towards me comes familiar face.
"Is it pleasure or punishment?"
He asks, bespectacled grin.
"Bit of both," grunts my reply.
"You plan a marathon to win?"
A chuckle and he goes on by.
Speeding motorist
Selfish pass.
I raise my fist and jump on grass.
Barking dog.
ON and ON and ON I jog . . .
Keep this up wind, rain and fog.
Summer's heat the hardest slog.
Blue jay squawking in a tree,
Mocking laughs at me.
Over the bridge;
Across the field,
Brambles, meadow-sweet, wind waving
In hedgerow greet.
Snails and pebbles 'neath my feet.
To aching legs I shall not yield.
ON and ON and ON I jog.
Sniffing hound trails after me,
Growls most threateningly.
Lifts his leg against a tree.
Makes me feel the need to pee.

Cyclist coming from the rear
Startles me
Flashing by so suddenly.
Their approach you never hear.
No panting breath for them
They just change gear.
Branches give a welcome shade.
The pace begins to fade.
ON and ON and ON I pound.
Why do I make this daily round?
To be the healthiest corpse
Set in the ground?
Snap! Yelp! Achilles tendon gone.
No marathon, this year, I've won.

USA/UK

I belong on two continents.
My life straddles the Atlantic.
"Hi!" "Good morning."
"Have a nice day. You're welcome."
"Will this rain ever go away?"
The telephone rings twelve times before reaction.
Four times and a machine springs into action.
Hold open a cupboard, close a closet.
Turn off a tap, turn on a faucet.
Bashed bumper, fender dents.
Write with a biro, use a bic.
You throw up and I feel sick!

MY LOVE

You stand there, slim in green,
Your hair neat helmeted
Moulds your head.
My 'star' shines softly on your dress.
Deep—deep—your thoughts
Arrange the quiet shadows on your face.
—Suddenly—a smile with pleasure curls—
Tears back the curtain.
Kindness, candour, laughter,
Set the day dancing.
No wonder I'm bowled over!

WEED

A weed is a flower
In the wrong place.
By God's good grace
I shall grow, my seed,
To be a flower,
Not a weed.

TENNIS

The net's too high.
The court's too long.
The sun's too bright.
The wind's too strong.
My feet are mired.
My eyes are tired.
I feel like lead.
That stroke is dead.
Throw away my 'HEAAAAAAAAD'.

TO A DAUGHTER

To my California girl
Who loves the sun, fun and
To socialize but underneath
Is very wise.
Slim and tall, beautiful.
A guppy child who loves
To swim, and ski and dance.
Mature at twenty-two who
Has given me, her mother,
Sound advice.
Made me see my life
In perspective, helped
Ease the pain of strife
Whilst living in depressed
And pessimistic mood.
Has shown her love and kind
Support to both her parents—
Who love her dearly.
We are proud to claim,
This youngest daughter.
The very best,
Our littlest pest!!

REJECTION

Words cannot express the hurt inside.
Brave faced I try to hide
The pain, the anguish and remorse.
Suffering must take its course.
You leave me with the briefest hug.
You are the source of my despair.
I cannot anymore this pain to bear.
It hurts me so to know that you
Are spending time with someone new.

THE MUSHROOM GATHERERS

Early morning, dew upon the grass.
Mushrooms springing at their feet,
Fast fed through nights by cows,
That patient breed, who grazing feed.
Black faced, ask, what do you want?
My milk? My mushrooms?
Chewing as they follow,
The morning gatherers mushroom browse.
Gentle lowing says, take my milk,
It is for you, spurting from the udder,
Fresh like the dew and the mushrooms too.
But the gatherers of mushrooms
Do not heed the cow.
With baskets heavily light-laden
They chatter home, across the buttercupped fields,
Trailing dewy footprints, home to breakfast.
Mushroom omelette, fresh baked bread,
Hot crisp from all night oven,
Spread with golden butter, jam or marmalade.
Tea and coffee with milk from a bottle
Goes into the cups.
And the cow still waits.

PHEROMONES

I am asking you to rebuild our marriage.
I have stretched the bonds to great length.
I have attacked your position.
I have injured your pride.
I have lacerated your emotions.
Can you forgive and forget?
Don't thrust a lance at my heart.
Don't keep pushing us apart.
Have the strength and courage
To give us a second chance.
Please heed my plea.
Hold me close to thee.

SUMMER OFFERING

Tayberry clinging to the wall.
Berries, red blue about to fall.
Netted to protect from birds,
Not for them to feast in herds.
Into the cage with bowl to pick,
Tayberry branches start to prick.
With juice stained finger
The berries are plucked
She doesn't linger.
Eager to taste the food of a dream—
A bowl of tayberries laced with cream.

ODE TO ME DAD

I am glad
My dad has come to stay.
We shall have some glee.
And maybe some sadness, too.
But you will see
That through and through
We really love each other.
Strange though it seems
We are compatible people
Even though I'm daughter and
He's father we can easily
Reverse the roles and let
The other take the other's place.
Two of a kind and yet two
Very different people.
Two twigs from one
Enormous family tree.
With him I love to be.

MOTHER IMAGE

My mother though an elderly lass
Is a real pain in the ass.
But to give her what is due,
She's a wonderful old lady, too.

"Sit up. Go comb your hair.
This dress is what you'll wear."
Hearing my voice like hers repeat,
"That's not the way to eat."

Beware I hear my children cry.
"You're getting like her, oh! how,"
They sigh.
Should I acquiesce and make no fuss?
Problems could be so much worse.

Children will fantasies relate,
With parent taking up the bait.
For years and years they thus relate.
And sometimes even come to hate.

Let tolerance begin at home.
So let them be, so let them roam.
The young are too prepared to fight.
Old fashioned ways not always right.

So I with patience bear.
Old lady rocking in her chair.
For, one day, that will be me.
Her likeness I already see.

My children I shall not berate,
For fear that they may come to hate.
And go too far away—
Never asking me to stay.

I don't want at later stage,
When in their turn as parents, rage.
See in themselves,
Reflections of their mother image.

MAINTENANCE MEN

The gardeners surprised me.
Weeds were whacked;
Blowers were blowing.
Mowers were mowing.
My visiting cat
Didn't turn a hair.
But me was I scared!

BETTER LATE THAN NEVER

In the autumn of his life
He took a second wife.
For three decades they'd loved
Each other and another.
An ocean distant,
Lives apart.
Separate days with different ways.
Joining briefly years between.
Companionable, compatible.
Short times to share.
Caring, loving and longing.
Feelings hard to bear.
Together now in gentler state.
Tis love for him, for her tis fate.
With hope they say, tis worth the wait.

TAPIR

Strange beast
Brazilian tapyra
Half dog, half hog.
Of the *genus tapirus indicus*.
As a pet they would cause a fuss.
Living in tropical America
Or the Malayan peninsula.
How do they choose such varying abodes?
They have flexible snouts,
To their forefeet four toes
And three to their hind.
Why, no one knows!
Naked with plated skin
Armored with brown behind.
They feed on plants.
Move about at night,
Have a nocturnal rite.
Cousin to rhinoceros.
The size of an ass,
For an heraldic beast they would pass.
Shaped so strange, tapir,
You'd cause a horse to laugh.
In the animal kingdom
You are God's farce.

MELLOW YELLOW

The pills were some delight!
I've been so ill tonight.
They did the works all right.
I up-chucked with all my might.
But I slept all through this night.
(Well nearly).
From 10:00 till 3:00 then threw up.
Went back to sleep till 6:25.
Woke up.
Started chewing rice krispies
Twenty times.
The *snap crackle pop* made me feel alive.
Thought I'd had a good night's sleep.
Next morning so drugged could hardly move.
I lost the use of my legs.
I swayed and tottered to the next support
Table, counter or person were my pegs.
I felt like the dregs.
MELLARIL!
It made me really ill.

COUSIN

I've got this cousin called Dave.
I think he's very brave.
And the family name he will save.
He was the only male left—
Until he fertilized the family tree
By the pro-creating of two sons
Andrew and Ian.
Fathered by a paraplegic
Who lived in a chair.
Dave doesn't remember
His Dad or his care.
His mother brought up two sons
All alone.
His brother, Michael, is dead
A sailor who died of cancer
At age twenty-two.
His mother has gone.
He's the only one left,
Looks to his family of cousins,
Aunts and uncles so he's not bereft.
A caring father, takes his boys camping.
Loves his garden and enjoys his job banking.
He's a solid branch manager of Barclays Bank.
Who after work likes to wallow
In the bathtub and have a brisk rub.
He has a good body
His physiognomy is fine.
I'm proud to say he's a first cousin of mine.

DEJECTION

It's been a fortnight since I wrote
No word not even a note.
I hoped you'd call.
No word at all.
Silence.
Am I lost to you?
Your concern for someone new.
While you sleep
I cycle fast the lanes
Of Lincolnshire.
By harvest reaped
And cows in mire.
My lonely vigil keep.
My thoughts so deep
Of you and time gone past.
Friendship, love to last.
My thoughts of you keep me awake.
I cannot sleep at night.
Will it turn out alright?
Maybe my letter you never got.
I'm waiting yet . . .
I cannot believe my plea
Could go unanswered,
That you think so little of me.
Give me a second chance
Not pass on by without a glance.

ODE TO THE OFFICE FROM A RECEPTIONIST

For ten months I have sat and looked at a wall.
Saved them at least a $3,000 haul.
(Health insurance).
The rest of the office
Gave me no recognition at all.
They would chat and converse
And often even worse
Be rude and unhelpful as well.
Bathroom trips were a nightmare,
For others quite simple,
They just went.
But for me a traumatic affair,
Somebody had to be asked to stand by
They would invariably ask why?
Great to work in an office
Where each thinks only of himself.
Ten months for me will suffice . . .
Susie, you're welcomed back off the shelf.

CHRISTOPHER

Have forty winks, my dear.
You sit sleeping in your chair
Hand to head
Relaxed without a care.
And I with pleasure watch
Your slumbered form.
Your knobbly knees,
Your hand tucked in your belt
Of zippered shorts, dark blue.
At rest.
The paper thrust aside,
Your glasses all askew.
Your bracelet on your arm
Tells me it's you.

CINQUAIN

Gardens.
Growing, green,
Digging, weeding, eating.
Peace, hilarity and God.
Abundance.

Daisies.
Straight, yellow-white,
Growing tall, glowing.
Honesty, sincerity, earthiness.
Marguerite.

Fish.
Bright, scaly,
Swimming, gliding, basking.
Too free to hook.
Reflection.

Cars.
Old and new.
Racing, throbbing, moving.
Maybe of use.
Transportation.

Moon.
Shining golden.
Gliding, peeking, smiling.
Cloud hidden, cloud clear.
Madonna.

Trains.
Huge monsters.
Puffing, chugging, sighing.
Get on, go away.
Railroad.

Delight.
Intangible, aware.
Taste, sense, smell.
With you all ways.
You.

CEMETERY

Garden of the dead.
Deaf, dumb and blind.
Bones laid bare.
Skeletons without a mind.
Moldering flesh and strands of hair.
A stone marks each corpse.
Wilted flowers. Despair.
Eagled entrance guards the way,
I dread the day that I'll lie there.

LINCOLNSHIRE

Another grey Lincolnshire day.
It is difficult to believe that
Elsewhere there is technicolor sky.
And sun.
The clouds hang so low
They engulf the distant trees.
So still the air.
No sound but tractors where
A field to brown earth laid bare.
To the sea flat, flat fens,
The dykes criss-cross the fields
Making a quilt of the land.
Grazing cows and scratching hens.
Farming country dotted with spires,
Deserted churches locked and cold.
No bells are tolled.
The houses show 'FOR SALE'—
Are never sold.
Why am I here?
I should be home
Back in the States
Where I belong
My family waits.
I shall not be long.

LOUISEE

Firstborn.
Our eldest child.
Beautiful and mild.
Her little sister's keeper,
Mother's helper,
Dad's delight,
The apple of her Grandpa's eye.
Rarely makes her parents sigh.
A social butterfly.
The telephone in constant use
Umbilically attached,
Her talking line.
A bonnie baby
Happy, a good sleeper.
A chubby hairless wonder
Who stole the other babies' thunder
By moving on her back,
Like a swimmer, turning just
Before she hit the wall.
Not very tall.
Petite and neat.
A snazzy dresser.
Happy to please
To be with people.
A cheerful kindly soul
Who gives her family love and support.

Sees her Mom and Dad as friends.
Marriage and children her likely goal.
The man who weds my eldest daughter
Will be blessed indeed.
May she have the life
She deserves to lead.

WILL-EE-AM

My son.
Named for his grandfathers
On both sides.
Will-ee-am, called by a surrogate
Grandmotherly baby sitter.
A lady with past experience.
He's the third in our litter.
Weighing in at ten pounds.
A big boy.
Sometimes a concern,
Sometimes a joy.
For him one's expectations are high,
On his cycle he'll cheerfully fly.
Not communicative, from him
It is hard to learn,
What it is that he thinks.
What it is that he wants
It is hard to discern.
Not his father's replica
He thinks he falls short . . .
With his mother he's fought.
I worry about his size.
But in his Mom's eyes
He could go far.
We want him to be happy
With himself and his life.

One day we hope he will
Find him a wife.
I love my son.
He's the only one.
He's our heir.

BOSTON

Pouring rain umbrellas up
People soaking, dripping hair
Sculpted to head, await
Wet but happy.
Anticipating in the rain
Riding on the train.
Ten minute wait.
The Greenline to the Hub.
Coins are rattling,
Quarters, dimes,
A dollar seventy-five
Jumping around as if alive.
Fed into the greedy maw
The ever hungry machine.
Like an animal without a claw.
Riding into Boston on the T.
In bound train for me.
RESERVOIR, a mother, child in arms.
RIVERSIDE, her baby calms.
BROOKLINE VILLAGE, an elderly man
With braid over one ear
And beard, his bag reads
Filene's Basement.
he's dirty and very bent.
LONGWOOD, girl in yellow slicker,
Looking like a fisherman,
Steps off, hood up.
She splashes her way through puddles.

The train draws on
And she is gone.
Improvements on the track.
We wait. . . . will I be late?
A sign reads—
"Creating jobs for today
Better service tomorrow."
Houses draped in vines,
Flower beds.
We wait, excited talking from the back.
KENMORE, a group alights to take a tour.
A black man sleeps, leaning head on hands.
FENWAY PARK, no one needs that stop.
Here there's baseball after dark.
Downtown Boston just a hop.

TO MY HUSBAND

You are the one I love.
We pledged a vow to one another
To love in sickness and in health
Until death us do part.
Please forgive me for being ill
Forsaking you and my family.
Don't keep breaking my heart.
I need you.
I love you.
I believe you need and love me, too.
Open your heart.
Come back.
Let us make a fresh start.
Who would believe at fifty-three
That one could be in love again with you.
You are the spice in my life.
Love with all the alternating
Aching misery and racing expectations
Of first love.
Let's see what it will be
After a sojourn with thee.

FORGETTING TO COME IN